INCREDIBLE
ANIMAL
FACE-OFFS

★ **ANIMAL** ★

HIBERNATOR BATTLE

RACHAEL L. THOMAS

Consulting Editor, Diane Craig, M.A./Reading Specialist

Super Sandcastle

An Imprint of Abdo Publishing
abdobooks.com

abdobooks.com

Printed in the United States of America, North Mankato, Minnesota
102019
012020

THIS BOOK CONTAINS
RECYCLED MATERIALS

Design: Sarah DeYoung, Mighty Media, Inc.
Production: Mighty Media, Inc.
Editor: Jessica Rusick
Cover Photographs: Shutterstock Images
Interior Photographs: Barrie Britton/NPL/Minden Pictures, p. 10; Getty Images, pp. 8, 9; Getty Images/iStockphoto, p. 5 (bottom left, top right); Perry de Graaf/Nature in Stock/ARDEA, p. 16; Shutterstock Images, pp. 4, 5, 6, 7, 9 (right), 10 (inset), 11, 12, 13, 14, 15, 16 (inset), 17, 18, 19, 20, 21, 22, 23

Library of Congress Control Number: 2019943328

Publisher's Cataloging-in-Publication Data
Names: Thomas, Rachael L., author.
Title: Animal hibernator battle / by Rachael L. Thomas
Description: Minneapolis, Minnesota : Abdo Publishing, 2020 | Series: Incredible animal face-offs
Identifiers: ISBN 9781532191947 (lib. bdg.) | ISBN 9781532178740 (ebook)
Subjects: LCSH: Sleep behavior in animals--Juvenile literature. | Hibernation--Juvenile literature. |
    Hibernation sites--Juvenile literature. | Animals, Habits and behavior of--Juvenile literature. | Social
    behavior in animals--Juvenile literature.
Classification: DDC 591.54--dc23

Super Sandcastle™ books are created by a team of professional educators, reading specialists, and content developers around five essential components—phonemic awareness, phonics, vocabulary, text comprehension, and fluency—to assist young readers as they develop reading skills and strategies and increase their general knowledge. All books are written, reviewed, and leveled for guided reading, early reading intervention, and Accelerated Reader™ programs for use in shared, guided, and independent reading and writing activities to support a balanced approach to literacy instruction.

CONTENTS

BATTLE OF THE HIBERNATORS

The animal kingdom is full of stars. But some animals stand out. These animals are the best **hibernators**.

Hibernators spend long periods of time in a deep sleep. This is how they survive the winter!

Animal hibernators are all around us. But what if you matched them up in face-offs? Which hibernator would last the longest?

WOOD FROG

ROMAN SNAIL

4

ARCTIC GROUND SQUIRREL

PAINTED TURTLE

FAT-TAILED DWARF LEMUR

BLACK BEAR

CHUNKY CHALLENGE

Black bears pack on the pounds before **hibernating**. Fat-tailed dwarf lemurs do too! But which animal would win a chunky challenge?

Large eyes to see in the dark

FAT-TAILED DWARF LEMUR
FOREST FEEDER

This tree-dweller is the world's only **hibernating primate**. Give it up for the fat-tailed dwarf lemur!

Long tail to store fat for winter

FAT-TAILED DWARF LEMUR STATS

HOME
The west coast of Madagascar

FOOD
Fruit, flower nectar, and small insects

NAP TIME
Up to 7 months a year

SIZE
About 20 inches (51 cm) long with tail

A FAT-TAILED DWARF LEMUR IS LONGER THAN A COMPUTER KEYBOARD.

FAT-TAILED
DWARF LEMUR

KEYBOARD

Strong sense of smell to find faraway food

BLACK BEAR
HARDY HIBERNATOR
This **hibernator** is a winter survival master. Put your hands together for the mighty black bear!

Bulky body to preserve heat and energy

Short, curved claws for climbing trees

BLACK BEAR STATS

HOME
Forested areas of Mexico, the United States, and Canada

FOOD
Berries, nuts, salmon, and small **mammals**

NAP TIME
Up to 7½ months a year

SIZE
Up to 6 feet (2 m) long and 600 pounds (272 kg)

A BLACK BEAR IS SMALLER THAN A CAR.

BLACK BEAR   CAR

CHUNKY CHALLENGE

FAT-TAILED DWARF LEMUR **VS** BLACK BEAR

FAT-TAILED DWARF LEMUR

A fat-tailed dwarf lemur's tail grows as it eats. By winter, the lemur's tail can be 40 percent of its body weight!

HIBERNATION STATION

Fat-tailed dwarf lemurs **hibernate** in hollow tree trunks.

THAT'S SLOW!

In summer, a fat-tailed dwarf lemur's heart beats 180 times a minute. In winter, it beats four times a minute.

BLACK BEAR

Black bears eat a lot in the summer. They gain four to five inches (10 to 13 cm) of body fat. This fat keeps them warm in the winter.

HIBERNATION STATION

Black bears make dens in caves. The bears add leaves and grass. This helps the dens stay warm.

THAT'S SLOW!

A black bear's heart rate slows during **hibernation**. It drops by more than half. So, the bears do not need to eat or drink. And they don't expel waste!

FROZEN FIGHT

Arctic ground squirrels are expert snoozers. Wood frogs are too! But which animal would win a frozen fight?

Short, strong arms for digging **burrows**

ARCTIC GROUND SQUIRREL
BRAVE BURROWER

This **mammal** rules the Arctic's icy underground. Get on your feet for the Arctic ground squirrel!

Stiff, thick fur to protect against cold

ARCTIC GROUND SQUIRREL STATS

HOME
Burrows in the open **tundra**

FOOD
Insects, berries, and mushrooms

NAP TIME
Around 8 months a year

SIZE
About 2 pounds (0.9 kg) and 14 to 18 inches (36 to 46 cm) long with tail

AN ARCTIC GROUND SQUIRREL IS LONGER THAN A LOAF OF BREAD.

ARCTIC GROUND SQUIRREL

LOAF OF BREAD

Toxic slime on skin to protect against predators

WOOD FROG
ICY IDOL

This forest critter can turn into a block of ice. Make some noise for the wood frog!

Brown skin to stay hidden on forest floors

WOOD FROG STATS

HOME
As far north as the Arctic circle, and as far south as Alabama

FOOD
Insects, spiders, worms, slugs, and snails

NAP TIME
Up to 8 months a year

SIZE
Up to 3¼ inches (8 cm) long

A WOOD FROG IS SHORTER THAN A PENCIL.

WOOD FROG   **PENCIL**

FROZEN FIGHT

ARCTIC GROUND SQUIRREL VS WOOD FROG

ARCTIC GROUND SQUIRREL

In the winter, an Arctic ground squirrel's body cools to below freezing. No other **mammal** gets this cold!

HIBERNATION STATION
Arctic ground squirrels **hibernate** in **burrows**. The burrows are lined with leaves and fur.

THAT'S COLD!
An Arctic ground squirrel's body temperature can drop to almost 27 degrees Fahrenheit (-3°C).

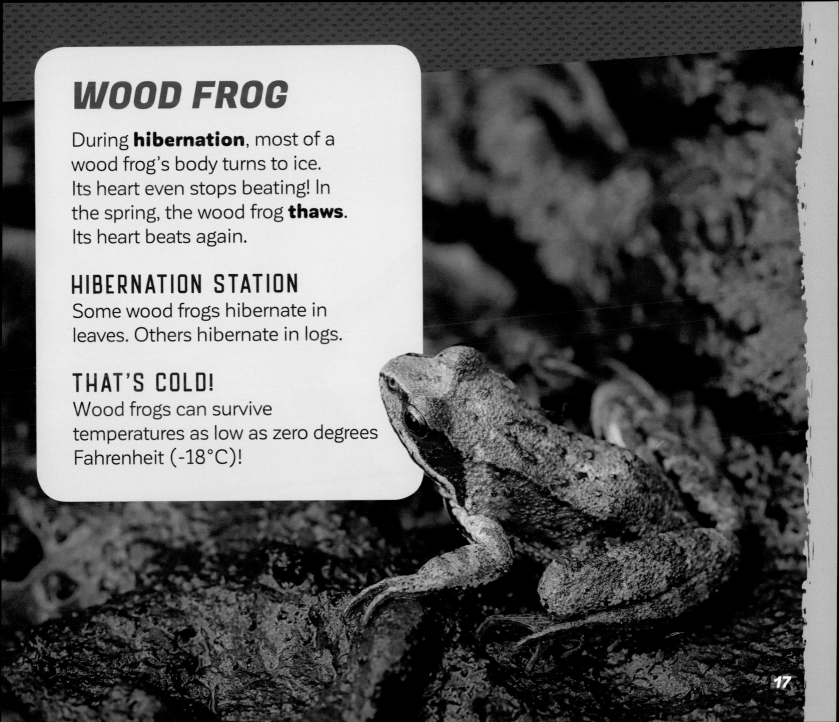

WOOD FROG

During **hibernation**, most of a wood frog's body turns to ice. Its heart even stops beating! In the spring, the wood frog **thaws**. Its heart beats again.

HIBERNATION STATION
Some wood frogs hibernate in leaves. Others hibernate in logs.

THAT'S COLD!
Wood frogs can survive temperatures as low as zero degrees Fahrenheit (-18°C)!

SHELLED SHOWDOWN

Roman snails are excellent **hibernators**. Painted turtles are too! But which animal would win a shelled showdown?

ROMAN SNAIL
SLIMY SLEEPER

This small creature carries its shelter wherever it goes. Give it up for the Roman snail!

Upper tentacles for seeing

Lower **tentacles** for smelling

One muscular foot to move

ROMAN SNAIL STATS

HOME
All over the world, especially Europe

FOOD
Fruit, vegetables, leaves, flowers, and tree sap

NAP TIME
Until temperatures are above 46 degrees Fahrenheit (8°C)

SIZE
About 4 inches (10 cm) long

A ROMAN SNAIL IS LONGER THAN A CRAYON.

ROMAN SNAIL

CRAYON

19

PAINTED TURTLE
UNDERWATER BREATHER

This scaly snoozer spends winter under sheets of ice. Say hello to the painted turtle!

Blood vessels to take in oxygen

Protective shell

Colorful shell patterns to blend in with surroundings

PAINTED TURTLE STATS

HOME
Freshwater areas across Canada, the United States, and northern Mexico

FOOD
Plants, insects, and small fish

NAP TIME
Up to 6 months underwater

SIZE
Up to 8 inches (20 cm) long with tail

A PAINTED TURTLE IS LONGER THAN A DOLLAR BILL.

PAINTED TURTLE

DOLLAR BILL

ROMAN SNAIL VS PAINTED TURTLE

ROMAN SNAIL

Roman snails seal their shells in winter. **Mucus** covers the entrance. This protects the snail from freezing.

HIBERNATION STATION
Roman snails dig holes in soil. They pull plants over the holes to stay warm.

THAT'S SLOW!
In summer, a roman snail's heart rate is 36 beats per minute. In winter, it is three to four beats per minute.

PAINTED TURTLE

Painted turtles can breathe underwater! They have blood vessels near their rears. These take in oxygen.

HIBERNATION STATION

Painted turtles **hibernate** at the bottoms of ponds, lakes, and rivers. These ice over. But the water underneath stays above freezing.

THAT'S SLOW!

A turtle's heartbeat slows underwater. This means the turtle requires less oxygen.

GLOSSARY

burrow—a hole or tunnel dug in the ground by a small animal for use as shelter.

hibernate—to pass the winter in a deep sleep. An animal that hibernates experiences hibernation. These animals are hibernators.

mammal—a warm-blooded animal that has hair and whose females produce milk to feed their young.

mucus—a thick, slippery, protective fluid.

primate—a mammal with developed hands and feet, a large brain, and a short nose, such as a human, ape, or monkey.

tentacle—a long, flexible limb on an invertebrate such as a jellyfish or squid.

thaw—to melt or unfreeze.

tundra—a large area of flat land in northern parts of the world where there are no trees and the ground is always frozen.